EMU LOCOMOTIVES

Mike Danneman

AMBERLEY

First published 2023

Amberley Publishing
The Hill, Stroud
Gloucestershire, GL5 4EP

www.amberley-books.com

Copyright © Mike Danneman, 2023

The right of Mike Danneman to be identified
as the Author of this work has been asserted in
accordance with the Copyrights, Designs and
Patents Act 1988.

ISBN 978 1 3981 0319 1 (print)
ISBN 978 1 3981 0320 7 (ebook)

British Library Cataloguing in Publication Data.
A catalogue record for this book is available from
the British Library.

Origination by Amberley Publishing.
Printed in the UK.

Introduction

Electro-Motive Corporation was established in Cleveland, Ohio, in 1922, designing and selling gas-electric cars (essentially a self-propelled passenger car) in the era of steam locomotion on the railroads. Even though it was a small enterprise, it caught the eye of a larger suitor. In 1930, General Motors bought EMC, as well as its supplier of gas and diesel engines, Winton Engine Co. It soon began developing a line of diesel locomotives requiring the blending of three controlling factors according to EMC's Richard Dilworth: physical limitations, engineering knowledge and economics. GM began selling these diesel switchers and passenger locomotives through its subsidiaries in 1935.

By 1938, GM's EMC was literally tooling its own future. Under one roof at La Grange, Illinois, the company was building its own standardised line of road and yard locomotives incorporating its own engines, generators and traction motors. The goal was to offer railroads a locomotive that was useful doing many tasks, lower in maintenance and reliable. At this point in history, steam powered nearly all of the freight tonnage moved in the United States. In November 1939, EMC waged a well-thought-out attack on this supremacy with an all-new FT, the first mass-produced road freight diesel. The olive green and yellow demonstrator set numbered 103 tested on the nation's railroads, pitted against the same grades and conditions that steam power fought for years. For eleven months, the 'experimental' 5,400 hp No. 103 racked up 83,764 miles through thirty-five states and over twenty Class 1 railroads to become what could be considered the most influential development in motive power since the beginning of steam locomotion.

On 1 January 1941, EMC and Winton were fully merged into GM, becoming Electro-Motive Division (EMD) of General Motors Corporation. The interruption of the Second World War put some restrictions on the manufacturing of the FT, but by the end of the conflict in 1945, railroads lined up to buy the new machines that were changing the face of railroading. Many of the nation's 40,000 steam locomotives were tired and ripe for replacement, and EMD quickly responded with a 2,000 hp E7 for passenger service, and a four-axle 1,500 hp F3 that could be used in either freight or passenger work.

By 1947, EMD employed 12,000 people and produced five units a day, overwhelming its competition. The company was so busy that it opened Plant No. 3 in Cleveland, Ohio, to build switchers and road switchers from 1948 to 1954. Refinements to the F3 led to the best-selling F7 model in 1949. In a short five years, EMD sold 4,221 F7/FP7 locomotives, decimating the numbers of steam locomotives still plying the rails. With a goal of making a diesel locomotive even more functional and utilitarian, EMD developed the GP7, a 1,500 hp road switcher marketed as a general-purpose machine. Selling 2,729 GP7 units between October 1949 and 1954 to seventy-four different railroads, an upgraded 567C engine soon ushered in the popular GP9 in 1954. Over 4,000 GP9s were built, pretty much putting US steam locomotion into the history books.

The continued growth of EMD added a Canadian subsidiary, General Motor Diesel Ltd. (GMD), and opened an assembly plant at London, Ontario, in 1950. In 1951, when Wabash E8A No. 1009 exited 'the home of the diesel locomotive' at La Grange, EMD finished building its 10,000th unit! The year 1952 saw the first SD7 built, the genesis of the six-motor Special Duty series that is still cataloged today – albeit in a much different form.

As a horsepower race began to develop, EMD introduced turbocharging, prompted by work done by Union Pacific. Both the SD24 and GP20 models had their 567 engine power boosted by turbochargers. In 1961, EMD introduced the 2,250 hp GP30, and the next year, it built its 25,000th locomotive – Louisville & Nashville GP30 No. 1014. The stylized cowling flowing back from the cab of the GP30 gave way to the 'spartan cab' design introduced with the 2,500 hp GP35 in 1963, and this cab design would last nearly three decades.

In 1966, EMD introduced a whole new line of 645-engined locomotives, including GP/SD38 and GP/SD40 models, and a big flared radiator 3,600 hp SD45. Full-width cowl FP45 units were specially built for Santa Fe passenger service, and a F45 freight version was added too. Milwaukee Road picked up a few FP45s, while Great Northern and later Burlington Northern added to the F45 count.

The popular 1966 line of locomotives was improved upon in 1972 when EMD brought out its popular 'Dash 2' line of the same models. Incredibly, 4,291 units of the 3,000 hp SD40-2 line of locomotives were built between 1972 and 1988. As passenger trains were nationalised under Amtrak, new locomotives were needed for the future. A fleet of ill-fated SDP40F cowl units were quickly replaced by a large fleet of F40PHs starting in 1976. In another controversial move in 1980, an effort to squeeze more horsepower out of the 645 in the 50 Series locomotives resulted in poor sales of GP/SD50 models.

Electro-Motive's bid on increasing its market share was the development of the 710 prime mover with the 3,800 hp 60 Series introduced in 1984. As these locomotives were built, cab design made for big visual changes. First embraced in Canada, the 'comfort cab', also known as a 'safety cab', was originally developed in Canada, and quickly became a standard in the US too. A three-window design in 1989 soon gave way to a two-piece windshield design on the SD60M. The first production locomotives with A.C. traction motors was a large order of SD70MAC units from Burlington Northern beginning in 1993. Union Pacific's historic 1,000-locomotive order of SD70M units in 2000 kept London busy in the new century.

From 1945 to 1983, EMD was North America's number one locomotive builder. With competition from General Electric and fewer railroads through mergers, orders were down. A gradual shifting of locomotive manufacturing from La Grange to the smaller plant at London was taken as a cost-saving measure. Even this wasn't enough, so GM finally sold EMD to the Greenbriar Equity Group LLC and Berkshire Partners LLC, renaming it Electro-Motive *Diesel* in 2005. In 2010, Caterpillar-owned Progress Rail Services purchased EMD. Both La Grange and London have since been shuttered and new SD70ACe-T4 locomotives are now being minted at a new plant in Muncie, Indiana. How long the EMD name will be around is anyone's guess, but it sure was a fun 100-year ride.

What follows is a selection of photographs that I have taken, of over 100 EMD diesel locomotive models, chronologically identified by model designation and years produced. Although not every EMD locomotive type is included in this overview, I hope you enjoy seeing the ones that are.

FTA—1939–45 EMD FT No. 103 from the original demonstrator set, mated up with a FTB unit, sits on display at a fiftieth birthday bash for the FT locomotive at the birthplace of EMD locomotives at La Grange, Illinois, on 17 September 1989. EMD hosted an open house in their honor, and displayed other notable locomotives as well.

E3A—1939–40 Atlantic Coast Line E3A No. 501 sits in the afternoon sun at Waukesha, Wisconsin, while powering an excursion on Central Wisconsin Railroad in May 1984. The locomotive was owned by EMD employee and diesel enthusiast Glenn Monhart, and later went to the North Carolina Transportation Museum in Spencer, North Carolina, after his death in 1998.

NW3—1939–42 Great Northern NW3 No. 181 makes a great display in the parking lot of the station at Whitefish, Montana, as seen on 6 September 1999. Only seven NW3 locomotives were built by EMD, all going to the GN. The units were built on lengthened frames and were equipped with Blomberg trucks, and had large cabs with a bulge just ahead of the cab containing a steam generator for passenger service.

NW2—1939–49 Union Pacific D.S. (diesel switcher) No. 1011 switches cars at Heber, Utah, on 9 February 2006. This vintage 1,000 hp locomotive was built by EMD in 1940, and served UP until 1977. The retired switcher went to Utah's Heber Creeper tourist railroad, eventually serving today's Heber Valley Railroad. In 2001, the locomotive was repainted in the as-delivered black UP switcher paint scheme seen here.

SW1—1939–53 Spiffy Amtrak SW1 No. 736 switches a cut of Amfleet and Heritage passenger cars out of Chicago Union station below Harrison Street Tower in May 1982. A total of 661 SW1s were built by EMD, making it the most popular early switcher locomotive.

SW1—1939–53 Advertising being 'Your Friendly Sand Man', green Dubuque Sand & Gravel SW1 No. 537 sits on the company's trackage at East Dubuque, Illinois, on 21 August 1994. The switcher was originally built by EMD in July 1949 for the Chicago, Rock Island & Pacific with the same number.

E5A—1940–41 Chicago, Burlington & Quincy E5A No. 9911-A, along with the *Nebraska Zephyr* Budd-built streamliner – both from the Illinois Railway Museum collection – rests in a siding at Burlington, Wisconsin, on the night of 29 September 1993. The E5 was similar to the E3 and E6 slant-nose models, but was customised for Burlington with stainless steel to match the railroad's Zephyr passenger trains.

NW5—1946–47 Great Northern NW5 No. 192 pauses during switching at Duluth, Minnesota, at the Lake Superior Railroad Museum on 10 June 2016. Only thirteen NW5s were built, with ten going to GN, Nos 186–195, equipped with Blomberg trucks and a short hood behind the cab housing a steam generator for passenger service.

NW5—1946–47 A short Massachusetts Central train with intermodal cars is tied up at the railroad's small facility on the west side of Palmer, Massachusetts, on 20 May 1993. Leading the train is NW5 No. 2011, a former Southern Railway locomotive.

SW7—1949–51 Peoria & Pekin Union Railway SW7 No. 407 is at the railroad's locomotive facility near East Peoria, Illinois, in March 1984. The SW7 model can be identified by having a gap between upper and lower sets of hoodside vents.

E8A—1949–53 Arizona Eastern E8A No. 6070 is freshly painted for excursion service in a short-lived Southern Pacific-style Black Widow paint scheme, as seen at Globe, Arizona, on 28 March 2010. At this late date, the E8 has been rebuilt and no longer has the four distinctive portholes along the side. E units, with two traction motors in each six-wheel truck and the center axle an idler, were almost exclusively used for passenger service.

F7A—1949–53 On 10 August 1985, a round-trip passenger excursion between Amtrak's St Paul-Minneapolis Midway station to Eau Claire on the Chicago & North Western's main line to Milwaukee is at Rusk, Wisconsin. Leading train is C&NW Nos 402 and 401, a pair from a fleet of 2,366 F7A locomotives built by EMD – by far the most numerous of the F units.

F7A—1949–53 Dressed in famous Warbonnet colors, Santa Fe F7A No. 347C and F3B No. 347B soak up some California sunshine in Old Sacramento at the California State Railroad Museum on 11 March 2001. AT&SF No. 347C is the only Santa Fe F7A that was not converted to a CF7 freight locomotive in the railroad's extensive rebuild program.

F7B—1949–53 Cañon City & Royal Gorge Railway's 9:30 a.m. passenger train is just west of Cañon City, Colorado, on the morning of 3 June 2011. The second locomotive on the train is CC&RG F7B No. 1503, and common to this model are the three portals along the carside.

FP7—1949–53 Canadian Pacific FP7 No. 1400 leads the Royal Canadian Pacific tour train at Fort Macleod, Alberta, on the morning of 22 September 2002. The FP7 is a 4-foot-longer version of an F7, with the extra length providing space for water tanks that supply the steam generator.

GP7—1949–54 A Soo Line freight pulled by a nice matching set of three GP7s approaches Shoreham Yard at Minneapolis, Minnesota, on 11 August 1985. GP7s are a 1,500 hp utilitarian road switcher with a workaday design that did away with the carbody styling of cab units like the popular F7. In their new model designation 'GP' originally stood for 'General Purpose', but they soon acquired the nickname 'Geep'.

GP7—1949–54 Over time, many GP7 and GP9 locomotives were modified by their owners, such as lowering the high short hoods to form a low nose for better forward visibility. Colorado & Wyoming Railway No. 102, painted in red, white and blue colors for the US Bicentennial in 1976, shows off its modified short hood. The locomotive is preserved by the Pueblo Railway Museum in Pueblo, Colorado, and is seen pulling a special train of two cabooses over museum trackage on 25 August 2021.

SW8—1950–54 San Luis Central SW8 No. 70 switches cars at railroad's small yard at Sugar Junction just east of Monte Vista, Colorado, on 6 August 1993. Common spotting features for this 800 hp model are the single exhaust stack and the six small louvers on the battery box behind the cab.

SW9—1951–53 Peoria & Pekin Union Railway SW9 No. 605 sits at the railroad's facility near East Peoria, Illinois, in March 1984. This 1,200 hp switcher looks similar to the SW8, but has two exhaust stacks.

SD7—1952–53 Originally Chicago, Burlington & Quincy No. 406, Burlington Northern SD7 No. 6054 sits stored at the railroad's locomotive facility in Clyde Yard at Cicero, Illinois, in November 1983. The SD7 model looks like a lengthened GP7 riding on three-axle, three-motor trucks, and are distinguished from later SD9s by their class lights being centered over the number boards, instead of toward the outside edge of the number boards. This new line of six-axle/motor locomotives was called 'SD' for 'Special Duty'.

F9A—1953–56 Rio Grande F9A No. 5771 glistens on the night of 25 March 1999, not long after being restored by the Colorado Railroad Museum in Golden in as-delivered Aspen gold over silver, four-stripe colors these locomotives received when built by EMD in 1955. F9As can be identified by the five vertical louvers present on the carside, with one of these placed ahead of the first porthole.

F9A—1953–56 A perfect A-B-B-A set of F9s pulls a loaded taconite ore train on a LTV Steel Mining Company's main line exiting Cramer Tunnel at Cramer, Minnesota, on 24 September 1994. The lead locomotive, F9A No. 4213, was later involved in a runaway wreck at Taconite Harbor on 13 January 1997. The train lost control on the 7-mile-long grade to the ore dock, with all four locomotives rolling over after hitting the switch that lined the train into a reverse loop, sparing damage to the dock. The engineer suffered a broken nose and ribs, while the brakeman escaped with cuts and bruises. Unfortunately, the locomotives weren't so lucky with the derailment, claiming F9A Nos 4213 and 4212 and F9B Nos 4220 and 4221, all heavily damaged and later scrapped on-site.

F9B—1954–57 Canadian Pacific F9B No. 1900 is providing more power to a passenger train at Banff, Alberta, on 1 October 2010. The F9B looks very similar to a F7B, but unlike the earlier model, No. 1900 has the F9-era Farr stainless steel vertical grills running along the roofline. Later railroad modifications include replacing the center porthole with a set of louvers to aid in engine room cooling.

FP9—1954–59 A westbound Keokuk Junction Railway freight switches yard at Bartonville, Illinois, on 7 April 2016. FP9s Nos 1750 and 1752 and GP20 No. 2003 power the train of cars for Kolbe station on this former Toledo, Peoria & Western line. Like the FP7, this model is 4 feet longer than a standard F9 to accommodate a larger water tank.

FP9—1954–59 After hosting a special trip, Kansas City Southern's 'Southern Belle' business train pauses briefly at Kansas City Union station in Missouri on the afternoon of 26 October 2013. Even into the modern hood unit-era, older locomotives like FP9s could still occasionally be found adding locomotion and color to a company business car train.

GP9—1954–59 A pair of EMD GP9s switch Union Pacific's yard at Council Bluffs, Iowa, in July 1983. UP No. 222 is a GP9 built in 1954 and does not have dynamic brakes, while GP9 (now labeled a GP9u) No. 332, equipped with dynamic brakes, as seen with the rooftop blister in the middle of long hood, is rebuilt with a turbocharger and now rated at 2,000 hp. Even though production of the GP9 model in the US ended in 1959, the locomotive was still built in Canada until 1963. An amazing 4,257 GP9s were constructed, which includes 165 GP9Bs, making the model the best-selling EMD locomotive up until this date.

GP9—1954–59 Southern Pacific GP9 No. 3392 pauses between tasks on a local freight at Stockton, California, on 6 March 1994. Built as SP No. 5653 in March 1956, it still retains much of the look of a standard GP9, such as the original high nose.

GP9—1954–59 Leadville, Colorado & Southern GP9 No. 1714 waits near the Leadville, Colorado, depot of the LC&S on the morning of 24 August 2021. The Geep (common nickname for these locomotives) was built in August 1955 as Northern Pacific No. 241, and later became Burlington Northern No. 1714 before its tourist-hauling years in Leadville. It acquired a low nose during a BN rebuild – a common modification many railroads did to GP7/GP9 locomotives during their service lives.

GP9B—1954–59 Union Pacific Slug S4 began life as cabless GP9B No. 316B that was constructed in September 1957. After the locomotive was retired in August 1975, it was rebuilt into Slug S4 for hump yard switching. Basically, a slug is a locomotive frame with only traction motors and added ballast weight, and is semi-permanently coupled to a locomotive. In this case S4 is mated to SD24 No. 446 for switching Bailey Yard at North Platte, Nebraska, as seen in the July 1984 photo. It still looks much like a GP9B externally, but has added large outside sand boxes over the trucks. A total of 160 GP9Bs were built by EMD, with UP buying 125 units and Pennsylvania Railroad acquiring forty.

SD9—1954–59 Southern Pacific SD9 No. 5399 sits in the morning sun at Lebanon, Oregon, on 26 September 2016. Originally numbered No. 5399 when delivered to SP in 1955, it was later rebuilt by SP into SD9E No. 4364. It was bought by locomotive dealer George Lavacot in 1992, who eventually restored and repainted it into SP's Black Widow paint scheme, with added silver trucks, and returning the locomotive to its original road number. The snazzy SD9 is currently leased to Oregon's Albany & Eastern Railroad.

SD9—1954–59 A Burlington Northern local freight powered by two SD9s flies along US Highway 2 east of Floodwood, Minnesota, on a sunny 19 October 1985. EMD built a total of 471 of these 1,750 hp machines, all of them with high noses.

SD9—1954–59 Duluth, Missabe & Iron Range SD9 No. 168 sits in the railroad's locomotive facility at Keenan Yard at Keenan, Minnesota, on 9 September 1989. Late phase SD9s like No. 168 featured some carbody alterations that will soon be seen on future SD18 and SD24 models, like a cab and high nose slightly higher than the long hood compared to earlier SD9s and two 48-inch cooling fans instead of four 36-inch fans.

E9A—1954–63 Union Pacific E9A No. 951 leads a UP OCS (office car special) westbound on the former Rio Grande Moffat Tunnel Subdivision as they smoke it up fighting the constant grade, and are approaching Tunnel 29 east of Pinecliffe, Colorado, on 19 June 2000. Both UP E9A Nos 949 and 951, as well as E9B No. 963B, were remanufactured in the early 1990s by VMV Enterprises in Paducah, Kentucky. They emerged in 1993 with new 16-cylinder 2,000 hp EMD 645 engines (replacing original twin 12-cylinder 1,200 hp 567 engines), with AR10 alternators and more modern GP38-2 design electrical systems.

E9A—1954–63 Burlington Northern EMD E9A No. 9922 on a BN/Metra commuter train rests for the weekend at Hill Yard in Aurora, Illinois, on the afternoon of 15 March 1992. Twenty-five former Burlington E8As and E9As were rebuilt in two groups by Morrison-Knudsen in 1973 and 1976 for service on the BN's Chicago to Aurora commuter route.

E9B—1954–63 Union Pacific E9B No. 963B is part of the locomotive consist for a UP Operation Lifesaver special out of Delta, Colorado, on 14 June 2009. Only forty-four E9Bs were built, mostly for the UP.

SW900—1954–65 Coors Brewing SW900 No. C987 waits for more tasks at Golden, Colorado, on 21 November 2005. This 900 hp switcher was originally built as an EMD SW in May 1938 for Rock Island, and was remanufactured by EMD into a SW900 in March 1958. The switcher went to work for Coors in 1982.

SW1200—1954–66 A pair of Kansas City Terminal SW1200s pull a train toward the narrows at West Bottoms in Kansas City, Missouri, on 14 September 1990. Just over 1,000 SW1200 units were built by EMD for use in the US and Canada.

SW1200—1954–66 Minneapolis, Northfield & Southern SW1200 No. 34 rests at Soo Line's Shoreham Yard locomotive facility in Minneapolis, Minnesota, in September 1984. The switcher was built in May 1965 and is equipped with optional Flexicoil trucks. Other options seen include a pilot plow, spark arrestors, modified handrails and drop steps to allow passage between locomotives.

FL9—1956–60 A Metro-North commuter train, led by FL9 No. 2002 in bright New Haven colors, waits overnight at Danbury, Connecticut, on 19 May 1993. Diesel were not allowed in either of New York City's terminals, but both had electrified third rails. These specialised F units were designed for New Haven to allow the railroad to power its passenger trains with diesel power, and then switch over to electric at the start of third-rail trackage into Grand Central or Penn Station. EMD lengthened the locomotive 8 feet from a standard F9 to accommodate electrical equipment and used a three-axle truck at the rear due to imposed weight restrictions.

FL9—1956–60 Powered by a pair of former New Haven FL9s, a Metro-North Commuter train flies west out of the Breakneck Ridge Tunnels near Cold Spring, New York, on the way to Poughkeepsie on the afternoon of 11 April 1991. These unique five-axle locomotives are equipped with Flexicoil trucks both fore and aft to provide room for the third-rail shoes. Looks like the rear shoe of No. 2020 picked up a blue tarp since departing New York!

GMD1—1958–60 Canadian National GMD1 No. 1421, along with GP9RM No. 7055, switch the grain elevators along Low Level Road at North Vancouver, British Columbia, on 26 September 2001. The locomotive is essentially a switcher with a lengthened frame providing space for a SW1200 hood, cab and short hood. Some GMD1s are fitted with A-1-A six-wheel Flexicoil truck, while others, like No. 1421, are equipped with two-axle Flexicoil trucks.

SD24—1958–63 A Fox River Valley Railroad freight heads northbound through Kewaskum, Wisconsin, on 25 March 1990. The train is led by the road's two SD24s, Nos 2401 and 2402, as well as former Southern SD35 No. 2500. After resisting the temptation to add turbocharging to engines for years, the 2,400 hp SD24 finally ushered in EMD's first turbocharged locomotive in 1958.

SD24—1958–63 Union Pacific SD24 No. 446, mated to slug S4, was hump yard power at North Platte, Nebraska, in July 1984. SD24s were available in both high- and low-nose versions straight from the EMD factory. They have a distinct blower bulge on the left side of the locomotive behind the cab, and above this is two more spotting features, a single exhaust stack and rooftop air reservoirs.

GP20—1959–62 Freshly painted Santa Fe EMD GP20 No. 3000 sits at the railroad's locomotive facility at Corwith Yard in Chicago, Illinois, on 22 November 1986. Prompted by Union Pacific research, EMD developed its own engine turbocharger, finally showing up on the new four-axle models with the GP20 in late 1959.

GP20—1959–62 The first GP20s built were for Western Pacific, and they had a high short hood, as did Great Northern's thirty-six units. On 25 February 1985, WP GP20 No. 2006 is stored at Salt Lake City, Utah, after its merger into Union Pacific in 1982.

GP18—1959–63 Toledo, Peoria & Western's Morton Switcher departs Morton, Illinois, with a diminutive train for the yard at East Peoria on a cold day in December 1983. The local is powered by TP&W's only GP18, No. 600, and only one car and a caboose trails the colorful locomotive. A GP18 looks similar to a GP7/9, but is equipped with a 1,800 hp 567D1 engine for power. Also, GP18s could be ordered with either high or low short hoods and with or without dynamic brakes, direct from the EMD factory.

GP18—1959–63 Central California Traction Company GP18 No. 1790 switches customers at Lodi, California, on 10 March 2006. This GP18 is a former Rock Island locomotive that is not equipped with dynamic brakes, but does have a high short hood.

RS1325—1960 Chicago & Illinois Midland RS1325 No. 30, along with EMD SW1200 No. 20, sit outside near the railroad's shop at Springfield, Illinois, in February 1984. RS1325s are essentially an end-cab SW1200 switcher on a longer frame with a GP18/20-style low nose and Flexicoil trucks. Constructed by EMD in October 1960, C&IM had the only two RS1325s ever built.

SD18—1960–63 Fifty-four 1,800 hp SD18 locomotives were built for Bessemer & Lake Erie, Chesapeake & Ohio, Chicago & Illinois Midland, Duluth, Missabe & Iron Range, and Reserve Mining. They were built with both high and low noses, and C&Os had trucks from traded-in Alco RSD-5s. DM&IR No. 193 shows off the lines of a standard high-nose version of the model at Keenan Yard, Minnesota, on 9 September 1989.

SD18—1960–63 Chicago & Illinois Midland SD18 No. 60 sits in repose for the night in September 1984 at the railroad's shop in Springfield, Illinois. C&IM owned two low-nose SD18s, Nos 60 and 61.

GP30—1961–63 In the late 1990s, a local freight ran west out of North Yard in Denver, Colorado. It still featured a vintage pair of Rio Grande GP30s, even though the railroad went from Southern Pacific to Union Pacific the year before. On Tuesdays and Thursdays, it would normally scurry west as far as Rocky Spur and Rocky to serve several trackside customers. On 20 November 1997, the West Local, powered by GP30 Nos 3006 and 3003, departed Rocky with eight cars for North Yard. The GP30 featured unique styling with a raised, curved casing running from the cab headlight to the front of the rear radiator grills, accenting a curved cab roof.

GP30—1961–63 Two Cimarron Valley Railroad GP30s sit outside the railroad's three-stall engine shop at Satanta, Kansas, on the morning of 1 March 2000. At the time, the CVR locomotive roster was exclusively colorful blue GP30s, including these two former Rio Grande locomotives still in their same road numbers. Just over 900 of these 2,250 hp locomotives were built by EMD.

GP30—1961–63 Soo Line train 11 leaves Duplainville, Wisconsin, on the afternoon of 26 July 1987. Power is a matching set of Soo GP30s, Nos 716 and 703. Gulf, Mobile & Ohio, Milwaukee Road and Soo Line traded in Alco locomotives on GP30s, and those units rode on reused Alco type B trucks with their original General Electric 752 traction motors.

GP30B—1963 Three Union Pacific EMD GP30Bs are stored at Council Bluffs, Iowa, in May 1984. Only forty of these unique locomotives were built, all for UP. Middle locomotive No. 731B is one of eight units equipped with steam generators for passenger service – rooftop vents are still clearly visible on the front end.

GP35—1963–66 Montana Rail Link GP35 No. 405 is at Helena, Montana, on 2 September 2003. This former Rio Grande EMD GP35 came to the MRL in this quasi-Missouri Pacific paint scheme of previous owner Omnitrax, and was later repainted in standard MRL colors. EMD's GP35 model is 2,500 hp, and features an angular, slant roof cab design (sometimes referred to as a 'spartan cab') that became standard on all EMD road switchers for over twenty-five years.

SDP35—1964–65 Southwest Portland Cement Company SDP35 No. 411 is running backwards (long hood first) with a train from Victorville, California, operating back to the quarry as it approaches Stoddard Wells Road on 5 March 1987. EMD's SDP35s are equipped with a steam generator at the rear of the squared-off long hood. SWPC No. 411 is the former Seaboard Air Line No. 1111.

SDP35—1964–65 Union Pacific SDP35 No. 1404 thunders west in eastern Nebraska with a train from the Chicago & North Western interchange point of Fremont in August 1979. In the 1960s, some railroads were facing the need to replace aging passenger locomotives with new power, but because of declining passenger revenue, they were hesitant to spend the capital. EMD offered the SDP35 as a way to provide the purchasing road with a new passenger locomotive that could also be used in heavy freight service. The locomotive is essentially a SD35 with its long hood extended to accommodate a steam generator. Previously, this generator could be squeezed into the high short hood of earlier models, but in a low-nose unit like the SDP35, there's no room for one.

SD40X—1964–65 By the early 1960s, the horsepower race was heating up and EMD had pretty much wrung as much horsepower as it could out of the enduring 567 engine. While developing the new 645 engine, it built several experimental units to test on various railroads. In 1964 No. 434 was built, looking much like a SD35 with three large radiator fans, and was the first locomotive powered by a 645 engine. In 1965 six more six-axle hood units appeared, numbered 434A through 434F. They also resembled SD35s, but had a slanted radiator similar to what will be seen on the new SD45. A single GP40 test unit was produced in May 1965 and numbered 433A along with two more SD40 test units, No. 433G and 433H, with this pair losing its flared radiators. After its stint as demonstrator SD40X No. 434 for EMD, the locomotive went to the Gulf, Mobile & Ohio as No. 950. It later became Illinois Central Gulf No. 6071, becoming an Illinois Central unit with the same number. Twenty-six years later, it was still hard at work, galloping across central Illinois as the middle unit of a southbound Illinois Central train between Ashkum and Danforth, Illinois, on 6 May 1990.

SD35—1964–66 The 2,500 hp SD35 can easily be identified by two large radiator fans with a small fan between, same as on a GP35. On 10 October 2005, Montana Rail Link SD35 No. 702 and two sisters are being used on the railroad's gas local out of Missoula, Montana, but have the afternoon off at the locomotive facility located there.

SD28—1965 A Cyprus Northshore ore train works upgrade away from Lake Superior at Silver Bay, Minnesota, along an empty County Highway 3 on 20 September 1991. The train is powered by a pair of rare SD28s, bracketing a trio of SD18s. All are former Reserve Mining, with only one fully painted in new Cyprus colors. Only six SD28s were built, with Reserve Mining getting four (Nos 1233–36) in 1965.

GP40—1965–71 A Conrail GP40 leads a westbound steel train at Tunnelhill, Pennsylvania, amid the autumn color of 23 October 1988. Conrail No. 3005 is a former New York Central GP40 of the same road number built in December 1965. A total of 1,243 GP40s were built by EMD.

GP40—1965–71 In the process of setting out cars is a pair of Milwaukee Road GP40s powering Soo Line train 243 at Duplainville, Wisconsin, on the afternoon of 12 April 1987. The longer 3,000 hp GP40 are distinguished from the GP35 by having three large radiator fans at the rear of the long hood.

SD45—1965–71 Departing Butler, Wisconsin, in March 1984 is a southbound (eastbound) Chicago & North Western freight led by a matching pair of SD45s. The SD45 can be identified by flared radiators, necessitated by the cooling requirements of the larger 3,600 hp 20-cylinder 645 engine. C&NW was the only railroad that acquired SD45s without dynamic brakes.

SD45—1965–71 Led by a rebuilt, battle-worn Southern Pacific SD45 No. 7464, an eastbound Union Pacific manifest freight train rolls downgrade out of Plain siding at Plainview, Colorado, on 25 September 1997. With its many mountain grades, SP was a good SD45 customer, also purchasing future EMD 20-cylinder models.

GP40TC—1966 An Amtrak 'Hiawatha Service' passenger train has just arrived at Chicago Union station on 1 March 1993. The train is led by unique Amtrak GP40TC No. 193. One of eight originally built for Government of Ontario Transit (GO Transit), these units have an SD-sized frame to provide enough hood space for an auxiliary engine and equipment that furnishes power for lighting, heating and air conditioning for the trailing passenger cars. Amtrak bought all eight from GO Transit in 1990.

SDP40—1966–70 For many years, Burlington Northern operated a trio of SDP40s on the branch to Golden serving the sprawling Coors Brewery – on trains called the 'Beer Run', naturally. Between trips, BN SDP40 No. 6398 rests outside the 31st Street locomotive facility in Denver, Colorado, on 18 May 1991. Once equipped with a steam generator inside the squared-off end of the long hood, the locomotive was built in May 1966 as Great Northern No. 324 to haul passenger trains. Only GN and National Railways of Mexico purchased SDP40s.

GP38—1964–71 Chicago Central & Pacific train 51 leaves Dubuque, Iowa, on 23 October 1993, with a pair of clean, red GP38s. The GP38 is a non-turbocharged 2,000 hp road switcher that racked up sales of 739 units in North America.

GP38—1966–71 Freeport-McMoRan GP38 No. 51 and three more four-axle locomotives work hard on a train of loaded acid tank cars curving through corral cut while climbing the steep 3–5 per cent grade from the Arizona Eastern Railway interchange at Clifton, Arizona, to the FMI facilities at Morenci on 23 October 2020. FMI GP38 No. 51 has some added options – special filters in the roof, a small fuel tank and reinforced pilots – and still wears the blue, white and red colors of former owner Phelps-Dodge.

GP38—1966–71 Louisville & Indiana Railroad GP38 No. 2001 sits at the railroad's Jeff Yard at Jeffersonville, Indiana, on 15 May 2014. Originally built as Baltimore & Ohio No. 3824, the locomotive went through several other operators before being rebuilt and labeled a GP38-3 and painted up in attractive Pennsylvania Railroad colors for its current owner.

SD40—1966–72 Missouri Pacific SD40s Nos 3088 and 3080, along with SD40-2 No. 3134, are at the Yard Center locomotive facility at Dolton, Illinois, on 15 September 1985. EMD's SD38, SD40, SDP40 and SD45 all ride on the same SD45-size frame, which results in large platforms extending beyond the nose and rear hood on some models. All of MP's SD40s lack dynamic brakes.

SD40—1966–72 A southbound Kansas City Southern grain train, led by SD40 No. 633, departs Kansas City, Missouri, at Air Line Junction on the morning of 15 September 1990. A total of 1,275 3,000 hp SD40s were built for North American railroads.

SW1000—1966–72 Coors Brewing Co. SW1000 No. C997 has just finished switching cars from the Commodities Yard to the East Silos elevator located east of McIntyre Street in Golden, Colorado, on 18 November 2005. This locomotive arrived on Coors property on 18 April 2003, and is former Burlington Northern No. 446, bought from National Railway Equipment.

SW1500—1966–74 Burlington Northern SW1500 No. 59 rolls through West Bottoms in Kansas City, Missouri, on the morning of 16 September 1990. Both SW1000 and SW1500 switchers have higher frames/walkways and have cabs with shallower, curving rooflines than previous EMD switcher models. The SW1000 has one exhaust stack while the SW1500 has two.

SW1500—1966–74 Denver Rock Island Railroad SW1500 No. 1083 crosses East 68th Avenue in Denver, Colorado, while switching cars working the Short Belt Job on the sunny afternoon of 30 March 2006. This is a former Southern Pacific locomotive freshly painted in the railroad's blue and silver scheme. The SW1500, as well as SW1000 models, could be purchased equipped with Flexicoil trucks, as seen on No. 1083.

FP45—1967–68 Atchison, Topeka & Santa Fe FP45 No. 90 rests at the Corwith Yard engine facility near Chicago, Illinois, on 1 September 1991. These EMD cowl locomotives were built at the request of Santa Fe, who wanted to replace old F units used on its passenger trains, and desired a locomotive at least somewhat 'streamlined'. Originally built as AT&SF No. 100 in December 1967, it soon went from passenger into freight service with the coming of Amtrak in 1971, and quickly donned freight locomotive colors and number series. With Super Fleet Warbonnet colors returning to the Santa Fe in 1989, the burly engine was again returned to a shiny coat of red and silver, and numbered 100. But the stardom was short-lived with the coming of new EMD GP60Ms in the 100-series in 1990; it was briefly again renumbered 5990 and at long last No. 90. The historic locomotive was finally retired at the hands of BNSF on 14 January 1999, and donated to the Oklahoma Railroad Museum in 2000.

SDP45—1967–70 EMD offered a 3,600 hp lengthened version of the SD45 equipped with steam generators for passenger service, with Southern Pacific and Great Northern picking up small fleets. In 1969, Erie-Lackawanna bought thirty-four SDP45s without steam generators, to take advantage of the long frame for a larger fuel tank. On 5 September 1995, a westbound Southern Pacific coal train drops downgrade on Tennessee Pass at Pando, Colorado. Leading the train is a former EL/Conrail SDP45 that MK Rail rebuilt into SD40M-2 No. 8695 for SP in the mid-1990s.

SD38—1967–71 Duluth, Missabe & Iron Range SD38 No. 222 leads a train of ore being loaded at the Fairlane taconite plant near Forbes, Minnesota, on 25 September 1994. A spotting feature of the SD38 is two large radiator fans at the rear of the long hood instead of the SD40's three. The locomotive recently arrived from sister road Elgin, Joliet & Eastern, and still wears EJ&E orange.

SD39—1968–70 Santa Fe SD39 No. 1567 shines in the afternoon sun of 1 September 1991, at the railroad's locomotive facility at Corwith Yard near Chicago, Illinois. Similar looking to the 2,000 hp SD38, the 2,300 hp SD39 is turbocharged and has one large rectangular exhaust stack.

SD39—1968–70 Soo Line train 17 crests Byron Hill south of Fond du Lac, Wisconsin, on the afternoon of 6 June 1987. Leading the train is Soo Line SD39 No. 6241 with nose lettering for short-lived Lake States, which was set up by Soo to facilitate spinning off a portion of the railroad to a regional carrier. The locomotive is former Minneapolis, Northfield & Southern SD39 No. 41.

F45—1968–71 Burlington Northern F45 No. 6613 sits on the wye at the locomotive facility at Chicago & North Western's yard in Butler, Wisconsin, in January 1984. This cowl locomotive was Great Northern No. 440, the railroad's last F45, that later went to Morrison Knudsen/Utah Railway.

F45—1968–71 Montana Rail Link F45 No. 392 pauses for a portrait at Laurel, Montana, on 11 October 2005. F45s are known as cowl locomotives, with the design likely reducing air resistance, but more importantly, it does provide a crew member some protection from the elements when troubleshooting at speed. Built as Burlington Northern No. 6642 in May 1971, the locomotive went through several owners before becoming MRL No. 392 on 7 April 1994.

GP39—1969–70 Copper Basin's unit train is westbound at Tunnel 3 east of Riverside, Arizona, on 18 March 2004. CBRY GP39 No. 505 is a former Chesapeake & Ohio/CSX locomotive. When initially produced in 1969, the 12-cylinder turbocharged GP39 was supposed to replace the GP38, but some railroads preferred a normally aspirated engine, so the GP38 remained in the catalog another two years.

DDA40X—1969–71 Union Pacific's DDA40X No. 6936 powers a westbound engineering special at Crescent, Colorado, on 4 October 2001. UP Nos 6900–6946 were called 'Centennial' locomotives in commemoration of the 100th anniversary of the driving of the golden spike at Promontory, Utah, on 10 May 1869, which coincided closely with their construction. At 98 feet 5 inches long, it's an imposing locomotive to say the least. A combination wide nose on a cowl unit-style cab, in front of a twin-engined long hood, over big four-axle trucks, the special-order UP locomotive is unmistakable. A pioneer too, as it also ushered in new modular electric controls that later became standard on the 'Dash 2' line.

SDL39—1969–72 A northbound Milwaukee Road freight passes the feed mill at Bixby, Minnesota, in September 1984. Powering the train are three of Milwaukee's unique SDL39s, essentially lightweight SD39 'branch line' locomotives, along with two rebuilt GP9s the railroad reclassified as GP20s. Milwaukee Road owned all ten of these locomotives that were specially built for the railroad's numerous branch lines with light rail and weight-restricted bridges.

SDL39—1969–72 An extra east Wisconsin Central train, led by former Milwaukee Road SDL39 No. 585, is climbing Byron Hill between Fond du Lac and Hamilton, Wisconsin, on the morning of 2 February 1992. The 2,300 hp SDL39 rides on export trucks with uneven axle spacing and is only 55 feet 2 inches long, making it even shorter than a GP7!

GP38AC—1971 In early 1971, EMD began offering the option of an AR10 alternator in place of standard D32 direct-current generator in GP38 and SD38 models, with these locomotives designated as GP38AC and SD38AC versions. On 20 May 1993, Central Vermont Railway GP38AC No. 5808 waits for a new crew at Palmer, Massachusetts.

GP38AC—1971 The Port of Montana is strategically located at the only place in Montana that is served by two Class I Railroads and two major interstates, 7 miles west of Butte, and as they like to claim on their website, it's 'where the rail meets the road'. They have there own locomotive too – bright green Port of Montana GP38AC No. 3641 – that can trace its ancestry back to Illinois Central, Illinois Central Gulf, Missouri-Kansas-Texas and Union Pacific. After switching the yard at Silver Bow, No. 3641 sits between jobs on 25 September 2006.

SD38AC—1971 Duluth, Missabe & Iron Range SD38AC No. 206 leads a train through Fairbanks, Minnesota, on the morning of 30 September 1989. Only fifteen SD38AC locomotives were built by EMD – six for Bessemer & Lake Erie, a pair for British Columbia Hydro and eight for the DM&IR.

SD45-2—1972–74 Freshly repainted Santa Fe SD45-2 No. 5830 sits at Corwith Yard in Chicago, Illinois, on 30 August 1986. Instead of reinventing the wheel, EMD improved its line of popular locomotives with the 'Dash 2' models introduced in 1972. Locomotives received mostly internal refinements like solid state modular plug-in electrical control systems, increased tractive effort and lower exhaust emissions. EMD touted forty changes and improvements made in the Dash 2 line of locomotives.

SD45-2—1972–74 A group of Montana Rail Link EMD locomotives are in various states of repair, being stripped for parts, or being stored in the railroad's Livingston Shops in Montana on 7 May 2012. Front and center is former Clinchfield/Seaboard/CSXT, now MRL SD45-2 No. 301.

SD45T-2—1972–75 Two southbound Southern Pacific trains sit in the SP yard at Mojave, California, on 3 March 1994. Both freight trains are led by 3,600 hp SD45T-2s, a locomotive commissioned by SP. The mountain climbing SP asked EMD to build a custom version of the SD45-2 that could perform well at high altitudes and inside the railroad's numerous tunnels. To meet these requirements, EMD designed a cooling system where the radiator cooling fans are relocated from the usual hot side location on the roof above the radiators to the cool side below them, pushing pressurised air through them instead of pulling hot air out. This 'Tunnel Motor' design gave the locomotive a much better and faster cooling system – just what the SP was asking for!

SD45T-2—1972–75 On the former Rock Island main line to Limon, Colorado, an eastbound Kyle grain train arrives at Seibert to do some switching at the Seibert Equity Co-op Association grain elevator on 6 May 2014. Kyle SD45T-2 No. 3099 is the recently repainted former Southern Pacific No. 9330, with trailing sister No. 9362 still in remarkably good SP paint.

SD38-2—1972–79 Chicago & Illinois Midland SD38-2 No. 75 sits near the yard office at Powerton, Illinois, in March 1984. Sister locomotive No. 72 and SD18 No. 61 are also in the consist. The 2,000 hp SD38-2, being well suited for low-speed heavy duty service, sold eighty-three units to mostly coal and ore haulers.

GP38-2—1972–86 EMD built a total of 2,222 GP38-2s for fifty-nine railroads in the US, Canada and Mexico, making the model a best-seller. Several hundred of them were customised to railroad specifications, such as Missouri Pacific's request for a four-stack exhaust system. On 23 February 1985, MP GP38-2 No. 2009, leading an Ogden to Salt Lake City freight, departs Ogden, Utah.

GP38-2—1972–86 A special train for Children's Wish Foundation of Canada operated over portions of the Canadian Pacific's system in the summer of 2011. Here, CP GP38-2 No. 3084 leads the special up Crowsnest Pass, British Columbia, and is headed into McGillivray Loop at a location now called Fabro. Standard GP38-2 models have two exhaust stacks that denote a normally aspirated 16-cylinder 645E3 engine.

GP40-2—1972–86 From the outside, a GP40-2 looks like the earlier GP40. But internally, EMD included a wealth of improvements into the Dash 2 line. D77 traction motors and AR10 alternator were refined. Improved bearings found their way into the 645 engine, turbocharger and camshaft, along with new chrome-plated stainless steel piston rings. A new electrical system featured solid state modular components. Useful on the GP40-2 model was an enhanced wheel-slip control giving the locomotive surer footing, especially important to mountain climbing railroads like Rio Grande, who ended up acquiring thirty-seven units. Powered by a pair of Rio Grande GP40-2s, Union Pacific's West Local switches the aggregates plant at the end of Rocky Spur leaving the main line at Rocky, Colorado, on 21 February 2002.

GP40-2—1972–86 Florida East Coast GP40-2 No. 415 leads a yard transfer across Jax Drawbridge over the St John River at Jacksonville, Florida, on 11 January 2015. Running on a railroad with no appreciable grades, No. 415 is not equipped with dynamic brakes. During this time, with the arrival of twenty-four new General Electric locomotives on FEC, groups of older power were no longer needed and the four red, white and blue SD70M-2s were headed off the property.

GP40-2—1972–86 A pair of Conrail diesels, led by GP40-2 No. 3344, hustle a westbound Santa Fe train through Houlihan's Curve climbing Edelstein Hill just west of Chillicothe, Illinois, on the afternoon of 4 June 1988. With Conrail in need of replacing older power, and the Dash 2 improvements adding reliability to a 3,000 hp model, it ended up acquiring 129 GP40-2s.

SD40-2—1972–86 Freshly painted Chicago & North Western SD40-2 No. 6848 flies along US Highway 30 west of Lowden, Iowa, on 16 April 1995. C&NW No. 6848 was built in March 1974 and nicely represents the features of early production SD40-2s. One of the spotting features of Dash 2 locomotives is the water sight glass seen on the right side of the long hood on these models, seen directly above the fourth axle on No. 6848. The SD40-2 model received all-new HT-C trucks as standard, replacing the SD40's Flexicoil trucks.

SD40-2—1972–86 Burlington Northern Santa Fe SD40-2 No. 8080 leads a train out of the crew change point of Sheridan, Wyoming, on the morning of 1 July 2002. BNSF No. 8080 is a former BN locomotive built in August 1979 and illustrates some of the modifications made to the SD40-2 during its production life. With 3,945 SD40-2s built by EMD over their long production span, the model practically became the standard locomotive of the late 1970s and early 1980s.

SD40-2—1972–86 A pair of Canadian Pacific SD40-2s rest in the yard at Field, British Columbia, on 18 July 2011. CP No. 5999 has an extended 102-inch nose that is frequently called a 'snoot' nose, and was often used by owning railroads to house equipment such as electronics for remote locomotive operation. During production, the SD40-2 was built with 81-inch noses prior to 1977, then switching to a 88-inch nose as standard. Optional snoot noses came in 102-, 116- and 123-inch lengths, likely dependent on customer needs and changes in regulations. The 123-inch length certainly fills up that big, empty platform up front!

SDP40F—1973–74 When Amtrak was ready to order its first new locomotives, it followed the lead of Santa Fe and looked at a cowl locomotive. EMD produced a 16-cylinder, Dash 2 version of the FP45 called a SDP40F and Amtrak was on its way to a new locomotive fleet. Officially unexplained derailments led to the locomotive's early demise, as Amtrak began trading in the model for new F40PH locomotives. Many SDP40Fs were scrapped, but Santa Fe acquired eighteen units from Amtrak in trade for twenty-five CF7s (road switchers from rebuilt F units) and eighteen remanufactured switchers. Santa Fe's 881 train storms through Wilbern, Illinois, led by freshly rebuilt SDP40F No. 5261 on 18 May 1985.

SDP40F—1973–74 A Santa Fe freight climbs the Arizona Divide west of Flagstaff, Arizona, on 8 July 1986. Leading the westbound train is a former Amtrak SDP40F, now labeled as a SDF40-2 by Santa Fe after being overhauled and modified for freight service by its San Bernardino Shops.

GP40-2LW—1973–76 Canadian National acquired a fleet of its own version of a GP40-2 beginning in 1973. Built with CN's own custom-designed safety cab that provides better collision protection, as well as crew amenities such as a refrigerator, hotplate and coffeepot, the GP40-2LW also has a lightweight frame to increase sand and fuel capacities without exceeding locomotive weight limits. As a result of this custom frame, these locomotives sit slightly higher than a standard GP40-2. CN ended up buying a sizable roster of 233 GP40-2LWs from EMD. Rocky Mountaineer Railtours GP40-2LW No. 8015 leads one of the company's passenger trains westbound at Banff, Alberta, on 3 October 2010. No. 8015 is former CN GP40-2LW No. 9635.

F40C—1974 Metra F40C No. 601 leads a westbound commuter train past Tower B17 at Bensenville, Illinois, on 3 March 1990. Similar looking to Amtrak's SDP40F, the F40C has unique corrugated side panels and is built on a standard SD40-2 platform. Bought for commuter service on Milwaukee Road lines out of Chicago, a total of fifteen 3,200 hp F40Cs were built by EMD. The first thirteen units were bought by and lettered for North West Suburban Mass Transit District, while the remaining two were lettered for North Suburban Mass Transit District. All fifteen spent all their lives working the lines west to Elgin and Fox Lake, eventually working under the Chicagoland commuter authority Metra.

MP15DC—1974–80 Kansas City Southern MP15DC Nos 4363 and 4365 pull two boxcars by the power plant approaching Oak Street on KCS's River Quay Spur at Kansas City, Missouri, on 16 September 1990. EMD's MP15DC is similar to the SW1500, but are 3 feet longer and ride on Blomberg trucks.

MP15DC—1974–80 Missouri Pacific MP15DC No. 1384 sits in the afternoon sun at the Yard Center locomotive facility at Dolton, Illinois, on 15 September 1985. EMD MP15DC locomotives built in 1975 and after are actually 1 foot longer (48 feet, 8 inches) than previously built MP15DCs to allow for larger stepwells.

SD40T-2—1974–80 Southern Pacific, still enamored with the Tunnel Motor concept it commissioned EMD to build with the SD45T-2 model in 1972, asked for a SD40-2 variant two years later. SP SD40T-2 No. 8355 waits on a train at the railroad's yard in Mojave, California, on 6 March 1995. The optional extended nose houses radio and electronic equipment used for remote-control helper operations. The SD40T-2 can easily be differentiated from its bigger sibling the SD45T-2 by having two radiator fan access doors between the radiators and lower air intake, as opposed to three doors on the SD45T-2.

SD40T-2—1974–80 If a railroad knew something about operating trains through the mountains, not around them, it was certainly the Rio Grande. On a railroad riddled with grades and tunnels, it took a page from Southern Pacific's playbook and jumped on the Tunnel Motor bandwagon. It placed five orders with EMD for a total of seventy-three units – ringing up a grand total of 219,000 hp worth of mountain climbing locomotives. On 22 September 1998, Rio Grande's first SD40T-2 built in October 1974, No. 5341, leads Union Pacific's Denver to Salt Lake City manifest freight at East Portal, Colorado.

GP39-2—1974–84 Initially missing from the Dash 2 line launched in 1972, the GP39-2 came into being from a request coming forth by Santa Fe. The railway wanted a four-axle turbocharged road switcher that would operate well at high altitudes, and the GP39-2 fit the bill. Terrain in Illinois is not exactly high altitude, but it doesn't stop several Santa Fe GP39-2s from gathering at the former Toledo, Peoria & Western yard at East Peoria in March 1984. Santa Fe ended up accumulating the largest fleet of GP39-2s, 106 units of the 239 built.

GP39-2—1974–84 The last GP39-2s built were twenty units for Missouri-Kansas-Texas Railroad in early 1984. Mechanically, they were GP39-2s, but externally the carbody was that of EMD's latest four-axle road switcher, the GP49. These MKT GP39-2s went to the Union Pacific with a merger in 1988, and several eventually were sold to Louisville & Indiana. Note the more modern grills and blower chute on LIRC GP39-2 No. 2378 leading a freight slowly out of Jeffersonville, Indiana, on 15 May 2014.

SD40-2W—1975–80 Under a stormy sky in Jasper, Alberta, on 17 September 2002 is Canadian National SD40-2W No. 5320 leading a westbound train through the yard. This 1979 GMD-built locomotive features the CN-designed comfort cab that provides better collision protection as well as crew comforts such as refrigerators, hotplates and coffeepots. This cab design became a CN signature for a decade and a half, and became the inspiration for all safety cab locomotives built henceforth for service in North America.

MP15AC—1975–84 Obviously a former Milwaukee Road unit, WAMX MP15AC No. 1598 sits at Columbia Falls, Montana, while operating for Mission Mountain Railroad on 7 October 2018. Soo Line's black patch 'bandit' paint job is so old that its former lettering number of 475 is showing through. The MP15AC is equipped with Dash 2 technology, and features a roof-mounted radiator and walkway-level air intakes similar to a SD40/45T-2 Tunnel Motor.

MP15AC—1975–84 Rolling along the Missouri River, an eastbound Southern Pacific transfer freight exits the West Bottoms area of Kansas City, Missouri, on the morning of 16 September 1990. On this model, Blomberg trucks come standard, making the MP15AC equally able out on the road.

GP15-1—1976–82 Conrail GP15-1 No. 1646 leads Housatonic Railroad train NX-11 through Brookfield, Connecticut, on 19 May 1993. Developed at the request of Chicago & North Western, the GP15-1 is essentially a road switcher version of the MP15, and designed to accommodate remanufactured parts from old GP7 and GP9 trade-ins.

GP15-1—1976–82 Former Chicago & North Western GP15-1 No. 4416 is now California Northern No. 105 at Napa Junction, California, on 7 March 1994. Similar to the MP15, the GP15-1 also has a cooling system that is comparable to the SD40/45T-2 Tunnel Motors.

F40PH—1976–88 Initially, EMD's 3,000 hp F40PH was designed for short-haul intercity and commuter train use. Amtrak's first batch of F40PHs, Nos 200–229, were purchased for some of its shorter corridor operations. Bigger SDP40Fs were to power long-distance trains, but this soon changed with the SDP40F's problems. More F40PHs were bought by Amtrak until they were the backbone of the fleet, becoming America's passenger locomotive. On 2 May 1992, F40PH No. 381 powers the eastbound *Illinois Zephyr* through Mendota, Illinois.

F40PH—1976–88 Regional Transportation Authority (RTA) F40PH No. 171 waits out the weekend at the commuter yard at Harvard, Illinois, on 26 April 1987. Metra (short for Metropolitan Rail) was formed in 1985, but at this time, much of Chicago commuter equipment was still in RTA colors. Other commuter agencies that chose EMD's F40PH to replace older power are New Jersey Transit and Massachusetts Bay Transportation Authority.

F40PH—1976–88 When Amtrak began replacing the F40PH with new GE locomotives, many went to new owners. After several years of leasing power from Amtrak and Union Pacific, Ansco, owner of the Rio Grande Ski Train, purchased a trio of the Amtrak units. In December 2000, F40PH Nos 242, 283 and 289 were painted Rio Grande Aspen gold and silver and began a second career pulling the ski train west of Denver. On 10 February 2001, the Rio Grande Ski Train curves toward Tunnel 1 just east of Plainview, Colorado.

GP40X—1977–78 Santa Fe GP40X No. 3801 basks in the afternoon sunshine of 30 August 1986, at the railroad's locomotive facility at Corwith Yard in Chicago, Illinois. Flared radiators are a feature of the twenty-three GP40X testbeds built as frontrunners of EMD's 50 Series, with these 3,500 hp prototypes carrying the new 16-645F3 engine.

GP40X—1977–78 On a rainy day in July 1981, Union Pacific GP40X Nos 9000 and 9001 sit at Council Bluffs, Iowa. Easily seen in this photo, flared radiators are a distinctive feature of the GP40X. Experimental HT-B high-adhesion trucks were used beneath ten of the testbeds constructed for UP and Southern Pacific, while Santa Fe and Southern Railway copies received Blomberg trucks. Southern's three units were also the only ones with high noses.

GP50—1980–85 A quartet of Burlington Northern EMD GP50s in tiger-stripe paint, spliced by a fuel tender, wheel a westbound intermodal train out of Chicago at La Grange, Illinois, on 7 February 1987, beginning its long trip to the west coast. The GP50 model made its debut in May 1980, without featuring high-adhesion trucks and flared radiators of the GP40X prototypes. Similar looking to a GP40-2, the GP50 has a taller radiator opening at the rear of the long hood to accommodate the cooling requirements of the 3,500 hp 16-645F prime mover.

GP50—1980–85 Missouri Pacific GP50 No. 3521, now cloaked in Union Pacific colors, rests at the Yard Center locomotive facility at Dolton, Illinois, on 10 August 1986. MP GP50s were the only ones built without dynamic brakes.

SD50—1980–85 A pair of Conrail SD50s, Nos 6729 and 6764, have run through to Burlington Northern's Clyde Yard at Cicero, Illinois, operating on the ELBN freight from CR's Elkhart Yard in Indiana on 22 February 1992. The SD50 model is powered with a 16-cylinder 645F3B engine and sits on a 71-foot 2-inch frame to house all the new 50 Series machinery, which includes a relocation of the dynamic brake grid forward toward the cab. This moved it to a cleaner and cooler location away from the prime mover, and did away with the familiar dynamic brake blister.

SD50—1980–85 Rio Grande wanted twenty more Tunnel Motor locomotives in 1983, but by this time, EMD was apparently no longer willing to build anymore custom SD40T-2s. After testing a quartet of Seaboard System SD50s in spring of 1984, Rio Grande placed an order for seventeen SD50s. Why the odd number of seventeen? A cost of $19.24 million for seventeen SD50s is the same cost budgeted for twenty SD40T-2s – of course! A southbound Rio Grande coal train crests the grade at Palmer Lake, Colorado, on 24 February 1986, led by a trio of SD50s.

SD50—1980–85 The SD50 model was plagued by low reliability due to engine failures, especially early in its service life. This is likely due to EMD wringing out about as much power as physically possible from the 16-cylinder 645 engine, and the model soon fell out of favor on several roads that purchased the locomotive. Union Pacific didn't order any SD50s directly from EMD, but amassed its fleet through mergers with Missouri Pacific, Rio Grande and Chicago & North Western. Union Pacific SD50 No. 5029 leads a taconite ore train through Little Lake, Michigan, on 19 January 1997.

GP15T—1982–83 Chesapeake & Ohio GP15T No. 1504 sits in Barr Yard at Riverdale, Illinois, on 10 August 1986. Only twenty-eight GP15Ts were built and are the only GP15s equipped with dynamic brakes – and C&O Nos 1500–24 are the majority of them built.

SD60—1984–91 Microprocessor controls and EMD's new 710G engine first appeared together in SD60 demonstrators EMD 1 through 4 between May and June 1984. Years later, the prototypes were still testing new technologies out on the road. Witness SD60 No. EMD 3 on the lead of a Burlington Northern Santa Fe coal train, now riding on a set HTCR-II radial trucks that will become standard on locomotives starting with the SD60MAC model.

SD60—1984–91 On the outside, EMD's SD50 and SD60 models look almost identical, minus a couple of minor details. Internally, the SD50 is 3,500 hp (later boosted to 3,600 hp in units built after late 1984) equipped with a 16-cylinder 645F3B engine, while SD60s are 3,800 hp machines with a new 16-cylinder 710G engine. Chicago & North Western bought thirty-five SD50s and fifty-five SD60s all painted in the railroad's 'Zito yellow' and dark green colors. A trio of C&NW coal trains are led by new SD60s at the railroad's remote yard at Bill, Wyoming, on 4 July 1989.

SD60—1984–91 Almost new, and the first of its class, Oakway Leasing EMD SD60 No. 9000 leads two sisters and a Burlington Northern GE C30-7 on a northbound BN coal empty at Palmer Lake on Colorado's Joint Line on 13 July 1987. A scheme similar to the quartet of SD60 demonstrators adorns the 100 Oakway SD60s delivered in late 1986 for lease to Burlington Northern.

SD50F—1985–87 Canadian National ordered sixty copies of its own custom-designed 50 Series locomotives. These unique 3,600 hp EMDs are equipped with a full cowl carbody and feature the innovative 'Draper taper', the so-called tapered notch cut into the cowl hood just behind the cab so the train crew has some sight line backward. This feature was the creation of CN Assistant Chief of Motive Power William L. Draper. After retirement from CN, several ended up on a couple of short lines. Montana Limestone Company's colorful pair of SD50Fs pull an empty cut of hoppers under the limestone loader at Warren, Montana, on the beautiful afternoon of 24 June 2016.

SD50F—1985–87 On the morning of 31 August 2018, Dakota, Missouri Valley & Western's wayfreight is southbound between Garrison and Coleharbor, North Dakota. Powering the train operating on DMV&W's Missouri Valley Subdivision is EMD SD50F Nos 5439 and 5408 bracketing SD40-3 No. 6911.

SD60F—1985–89 Quickly following Canadian National's purchase of the unique SD50Fs, CN ordered more cowl locomotives in the form of sixty-four 60 Series 710G-engined EMD SD60Fs. On 11 July 2014, CN SD60F No. 5518 leads a second section of CN train 847 through Jasper National Park at Henry House, Alberta.

F40PH-2—1985–89 VIA's eastbound train 2, the *Canadian*, leaves Jasper at English, Alberta, running over Canadian National's main line on 18 September 2002. Two F40PH-2s power the twenty-one-car train, with No. 6441 leading the way. Other than having 3,200 hp, EMD's F40PH-2 is identical to the earlier F40PH.

GP60—1985–94 The most powerful Geep ever, at 3,800 hp, the new 60 Series GP60 made their debut in October 1985 when EMD sent a trio of blue and white demonstrators on an impressive continental tour. EMD Nos 5, 6 and 7 fly eastbound on the Santa Fe main line approaching Toluca, Illinois, on 19 April 1986. The rounded contours of the cab and nose were not repeated on regular production GP60s.

GP60—1985–94 Southern Pacific was the first railroad to actually purchase GP60s in December 1987. A westbound SP freight climbs the former Rio Grande route over Soldier Summit between Colton and Summit, Utah, on the afternoon of 7 September 1995.

GP60—1985–94 Even though the SD60 model was outselling the GP60 three to one, EMD still racked up sales of 294 GP60s, including three to Rio Grande, the railroad's last new locomotives. Black and Aspen gold GP60 No. 3155 leads Ansco's Rio Grande Ski Train around the wye at Tabernash, Colorado, on 22 March 1997.

SD40-2F—1988 Canadian Pacific had the third largest bought-new fleet of SD40-2s in North America, behind Burlington Northern and Union Pacific. More than two years after EMD built its last SD40-2 for Nationales de Mexico, CP came knocking on EMD's door for more. They obliged, but the locomotives built were no ordinary Dash 2s, as CP took delivery of twenty-five big red custom-built cowl units labeled SD40-2Fs. A great way to put a capstone on 5,752 3,000 hp 645-powered C-C locomotives!

F59PH—1988–94 The F59PH was commissioned and cooperatively designed with Ontario's Toronto area commuter agency Go Transit. A full-cowl 3,000 hp locomotive fitted with a 710G3 engine and equipped with a Canadian National-style cab, EMD ended up building seventy-two of the four-axle passenger units. After serving GO Transit, six F59PHs went to Chicago's Metra. On the morning of 9 November 2017, two Metra commuter trains make their way into Chicago Union station passing Taylor Street in Chicago, Illinois. The two inbounds are powered by F40PHM-2 No. 213 and former GO Transit F59PH No. 99.

F69PHAC—1989 Amtrak F69PHAC Nos 450 and 451 were the first all-new A.C. traction locomotives in North America. They were experimental locomotives in a carbody similar to a F40PH, but with a built-out windshield sloping back from the nose, and were outfitted with Siemens A.C. traction equipment along with a 12-cylinder 710G engine. After evaluation at Pueblo's test track, they put on thousands of miles in passenger service, providing EMD with plenty of test data and real road experience using A.C. traction. Having served their purpose as testbeds, the pair returned to EMD (and later briefly toured with Amtrak's ICE train) and finally succumbed to languishing unused at NRE after 1999. In this view, the pair kicks up some dust leading Amtrak's Empire Builder through Pewaukee, Wisconsin, on the afternoon of 31 May 1992.

SD60M—1989–93 The first EMD locomotive equipped with the new wide-nose 'North American cab', also commonly called a comfort cab, made its appearance in January 1989 when Union Pacific SD60M No. 6085 was outshopped from the EMD plant at London, Ontario. The new cabs quickly became standard, with the 'M' in SD60M standing for 'modified'. With a friendly wave from the cab, Soo Line train 203 passes the shore of Pewaukee Lake at Pewaukee, Wisconsin, on the nice autumn day of 6 October 1990. An EMD SD60M/SD60 combo in Soo's new candy apple red powers the westbound hotshot.

SD60M—1989–93 Passing through the stark landscape of the Badlands in North Dakota, a westbound Burlington Northern coal train exits the siding at Sully Springs on the afternoon of 9 August 1991. The empties heading back to Powder River Basin are powered by three fresh SD60Ms and an older SD40-2. BN acquired 100 Cascade green SD60Ms from EMD.

SD60M—1989–93 Brand-new Union Pacific SD60M Nos 6194 and 6205 are in the final stages of assembly as they are 'trucked' with an overhead crane specially for visitors during an open house at the sprawling EMD plant at La Grange, Illinois, on 17 September 1989.

SD60M—1989–93 EMD redesigned the North American cab in late 1990. The new cab now featured two teardrop windows and a modified nose to provide better visibility of a crewman on the front stepwell. The new cab was introduced in January 1991 with the first locomotives of a second fifty-unit order of Burlington Northern SD60Ms. In this photo, BN SD60M No. 9276 shows off its two-piece windshield and reshaped nose while leading Amtrak's *Southwest Chief* at Glorieta, New Mexico, on 20 May 1999. Apparently some power issues occurring further east on the trip had required the assistance of an additional freight locomotive. BN No. 9276 plays follow the leader to a quartet of Amtrak GE P42DCs, all tagging along on the twenty-two-car train.

GP60M—1990 Santa Fe commissioned custom-designed comfort cab-equipped GP60Ms from EMD, delivered in 1990. A trio of EMD GP60Ms, Nos 150, 111 and 137, round Houlihan's Curve just west of Chillicothe, Illinois, at 4:30 p.m. on 24 August 1991. This is Santa Fe's 199 train, and it is getting up to a good speed for the short grind over Edelstein Hill. The hottest of the hot, the 199 train was a premium Chicago to the Richmond, California, piggyback, and always rated some of the newest power on the railway.

GP60M—1990 In addition to the sixty-three GP60Ms in revived 'Super Fleet' Warbonnet colors that Santa Fe bought in 1990, twenty-three additional GP60s came online in 1991. These cabless GP60Bs were only produced for Santa Fe, and were also painted in classic red and silver colors. A perfect complement to the GP60M, these 'B units' could be occasionally found splicing a pair of GP60Ms, forming A-B-A or A-B-B-A locomotive consists, echoing vintage F unit lash-ups of Santa Fe's illustrious past. After the BNSF merger, the GP60Bs were eventually repainted into BNSF colors, like No. 346 running in the locomotive consist of BNSF's Chewelah Turn rumbling through Denison, Washington, on a sunny 23 February 2017.

GP60B—1991 Predecessor Santa Fe could put together some awesome consists with their GP60M and GP60B locomotives, but BNSF could put some terrific ones together too. An impressive EMD A-B-B-B-B-A set of GP60M No. 105, GP60B Nos 331, 335, 344 and 336, and GP50 No. 3120 on BNSF's Chewelah Turn is seen passing a recently harvested wheat field approaching Deer Park, Washington, on 12 October 2018.

SD60MAC—1991–92 A quartet of SD60MACs were built by EMD to test Siemens' alternating current traction equipment and the builder's HTCR-II radial (steerable) truck. Constructed on a 74-foot frame, the 3,800 hp SD60MAC was painted in a unique Burlington Northern Cascade green and white scheme, with both BN and EMD lettering, and numbered 9500–9503. Soo Line tested the SD60MACs in 1993, and in this view, Nos 9500, 9503 and 9502 are leading Soo Line train 430 at Green Island, Iowa, on a dreary 17 October 1993.

SD60MAC—1991–92 A westbound Burlington Northern Santa Fe coal empty descends Crawford Hill east of Crawford, Nebraska, on the morning of 11 April 1998. A short-lived mix of A.C. locomotives power the train back toward another load of Powder River coal. Leading is BN SD60MAC No. 9501 dressed in its BN/EMD demonstrator colors, new orange BNSF SD70MAC No. 9844 and BN SD70MAC No. 9648.

BL20-2—1992 Burlington Northern train 101 rumbles through Budd, Illinois, on 21 August 1994, led by a rare BL20-2 locomotive. Three BL20-2s were built on the frames of former BN GP9s, and featured a rebuilt turbocharged 16-567 engine rated at 2,000 hp, mated with an AR10 alternator and a Dash 2 electrical system, along with an all-new cab and carbody. The unique prototype units were built by EMD in 1992 and were numbered 120–122, but EMD garnered no orders for the locomotives.

F40PHM-2—1992–93 Metra F40PHM-2 is at Aurora, Illinois, on 15 March 1992. Chicago's regional commuter authority, Metra, bought thirty of these units in 1991–92. The 3,200 hp locomotive is no different mechanically than a F40PH-2, but the streamlined cab and built-out windows give them a distinctive profile. For some, the unique slanted windows and lack of a front nose gave the locomotives the informal nickname 'Winnebagos' after the popular line of similar-looking recreational vehicles. As an aside, Metra F40PHM-2 No. 214 was the last locomotive assembled at La Grange, outshopped in December 1992. Thereafter, EMD locomotive construction shifted to the London, Ontario, plant.

F40PHM-2—1992–93 On a snowy 11 November 2019, an outbound Metra commuter train led by EMD F40PHM-3 (rebuilt by Metra to a 'Dash 3') No. 192 passes CP Taylor south of Chicago Union Station.

SD70M—1992–2004 Sales of SD70Ms from the 70 Series were slow at first, with a lot of floor space at EMD devoted to erecting A.C. traction SD70MACs. One exception was a small order of twenty-five SD70Ms for Southern Pacific in 1994. On 11 December 1994, new SP SD70M No. 9814 leads an ore train on Wisconsin Central at North Fond du Lac, Wisconsin.

SD70M—1992–2004 The largest single-model locomotive order ever placed in North America was Union Pacific's historic 1,000-unit reservation for SD70Ms in October 1999. Delivered over a period of four years, the SD70M evolved slightly as new regulations took effect as different groups were constructed. In addition, there were so many locomotives to be built that EMD used some contract shops to help with the work. UP SD70M No. 4145 leading the railroad's MRONY freight west of Clay, Colorado, on 23 April 2001 was one of forty-six units built for EMD at Super Steel Schenectady Inc. in Glenville, New York.

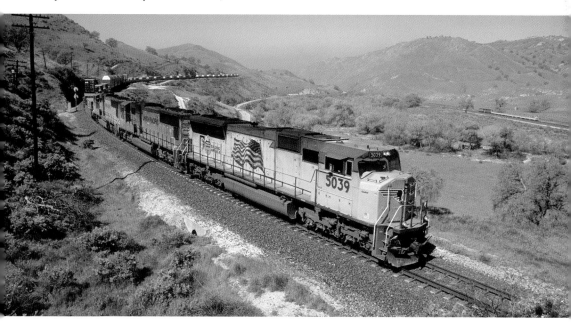

SD70M—1992–2004 Needing to comply with approaching Tier 1 emissions standards in 2002, EMD beefed up the cooling system of the SD70M model. In doing so, the new larger split-cooling radiators necessitated bigger flared radiators reminiscent of the SD45. These flared radiators became standard in the Tier 1-compliant units beginning in 2002. Working over Tehachapi Pass, a trio of SD70Ms power a northbound UP train downgrade into Caliente, California, on 11 March 2005. Lead SD70M No. 5039 was built in September 2002 and its flared radiators can easily be seen.

SD70M—1992–2004 Two SD70Ms wait for work at Union Pacific's Downing B. Jenks Shop in North Little Rock, Arkansas, on 19 May 2015. No. 5090 has the 'standard' SD70M cab, while sister No. 5155 is equipped with a so-called Phase II cab with the same windshields, but has a nose with sharper features and a raised center portion accommodating a full-size door – a similar look that foretold the SD70ACe. Including the twenty-five units from Southern Pacific, UP added 1,454 SD70Ms to its roster!

SD70—1993–94 Even though the comfort cab was standard on 70 Series locomotives, Norfolk Southern, Illinois Central and Conrail (under NS guidance in anticipation of the Conrail break-up) acquired conventional-cab SD70s. On 2 August 2005, NS SD70 No. 2550 is being used on the Canadian National at Sussex, Wisconsin.

SD60I—1993–95 EMD continued to improve its design of the North American cab (also known as a comfort cab) when it unveiled the 'WhisperCab' on Conrail SD60I No. 5544 in April 1993. Designed to improve noise and vibration, the 'I' for 'isolated' cab rides on a cushion of rubber mounts that isolates it from the frame and hood of the locomotive. Conrail's eighty SD60Is were the only ones built, and forty-six went to Norfolk Southern with the Conrail acquisition (split with CSX) on 1 June 1999. Led by NS SD60I No. 6757, NS train 38Q smokes it up going through Vance, Tennessee, on the NS's Knoxville East End District on 13 May 2014.

SD70MAC—1993–2004 On 23 May 1997, at the east end of Alliance Yard, a coal load departs eastbound for the Sand Hills Subdivision while three others wait their turn. Heavy BNSF coal trains in this era are the domain of EMD's A.C.-powered SD70MACs, as seen on this damp spring day in Nebraska.

SD70MAC—1993–2004 The SD60MACs that EMD painted for Burlington Northern were tested thoroughly, and the merits of A.C. traction burgeoned. BN signed a $675 million order for 350 4,000 hp A.C. traction SD70MACs from EMD, sight unseen, based on the SD60MAC's performance on the road. With that simple stroke of the pen, the A.C. revolution was underway. On 6 July 2001, BN SD70MAC No. 9702 leads a westbound unit coal train on Montana Rail Link at Livingston, Montana. BN SD70MACs were commonly called 'Grinsteins' after BN Chairman Gerald Grinstein, who was influential in the development of BN's final paint scheme.

SD70MAC—1993–2004 A group of Burlington Northern Santa Fe SD70MACs share floor space in the diesel shop at Alliance, Nebraska, on 21 July 2003. Hauling hulking trains of coal takes its toll on these hard-working machines.

SD70MAC—1993–2004 Six EMD SD70MACs lead a westbound Burlington Northern Santa Fe coal train west on Union Pacific's Moffat Tunnel Subdivision at Rollinsville, Colorado, on 3 October 2001. Before the train loaded with Utah coal heads east, the extra locomotives up front will be set up as mid and rear DPUs (distributed power units). All 70 Series six-axle locomotives have EMD's HTCR-II truck as standard.

SD70MAC—1993–2004 BNSF SD70MAC No. 9879 heads a westbound coal train past the shore of Barr Lake at Barr, Colorado, on the morning of 26 November 2010. After the Burlington Northern and Santa Fe merger, BNSF continued to purchase more SD70MACs from EMD, amassing a fleet of 786 units!

F59PHI—1994–2001 EMD's F59PHI is pretty much a full-cowl F59PH with a streamlined cab and fiberglass nose. Also unique to the model are side skirts over the fuel tank and a smooth roof profile to match with bi-level California passenger cars, so the locomotives are sometimes referred to as 'California F59s'. Two Amtrak capital corridor trains meet at Davis, California, on a rainy 14 March 2006. CDTX (California Department of Transportation) F59PHI Nos 2001 and 2013 power the trains.

F59PHI—1994–2001 Eleven F59PHI locomotives found a home on Seattle's Sound Transit Sounder commuter trains during 1999–2001. Heading northbound at Richmond Beach at Shoreline, Washington, on 30 June 2006 is a Sounder commuter train powered by SNDX No. 911, specially painted in 'Homerun Service' for the Seattle Mariners Major League baseball team.

SD70I—1995 Equipped with EMD's top of the line WhisperCab, Canadian National's twenty-six SD70Is built in July to November 1995 are the only 70 Series built with the isolated cab feature. Surrounded by the rugged mountains inside Jasper National Park, CN SD70I No. 5723 leads train 417 through Henry House, Alberta, on the morning of 10 July 2014.

SD75M—1995–96 EMD's SD75M bears a close resemblance to its SD70M predecessor, but internally, the horsepower went from 4,000 to 4,300 with the SD75M. Santa Fe and BNSF received the only SD75Ms built, Santa Fe Nos 200 to 250, and BNSF Nos 8251 to 8275. Warbonnet BNSF SD75M No. 8267, built by EMD in February 1996, sits in the siding at Ash Hill, California, on 11 March 2002.

SD75M—1995–96 An eastbound BNSF freight has just crossed the Washington-Idaho state line and approaches Hauser Yard at Hauser Junction, Idaho, on 6 October 2018. A pair of good-looking EMDs power the train – SD75M No. 258, formerly a warbonnet-clad BNSF No. 8258, and SD60M No. 1412 that was Cascade green Burlington Northern No. 9225 in a previous life.

SD90MAC—1995–2000 There was a perceived horsepower race in the early 1990s, and EMD (and GE) even took orders for a 6,000 hp locomotive that didn't even exist yet. EMD's SD90MAC is an 80-foot 2-inch giant, with oversized radiators and dynamic brakes placed behind them at the rear of the long hood. The first SD90MACs would be built with 4,300 hp 16-710G3 engines to eventually be repowered with EMD's new 6,000 hp 265H prime mover when it was put into production. Only Union Pacific, Canadian Pacific and CEFX (leasing company) received these 4,300 hp SD90MACs that UP labeled a SD9043MAC, and are sometimes called 'convertibles'. Canadian Pacific bought sixty-one SD90MACs, like CP No. 9141 resting in the yard at Field, British Columbia, on the afternoon of 16 September 2002.

SD90MAC—1995–2000 As development of the 6,000 hp 265H engine dragged on, the 'upgradable' 4,300 hp SD90MAC carried on, as the 710-powered SD90MAC is essentially an A.C. version of the proven SD75I. As it turns out, none of the 410 4,300 hp SD90MACs were ever converted to 6,000 hp! A westbound Canadian Pacific grain train led by two UP SD90MAC (SD9043MAC) locomotives approaches historic Crowsnest Pass, Alberta, on 28 September 2010.

SD75I—1996–99 Beyond its isolated cab, the SD75I is pretty much identical to a SD75M. The way to tell the difference between the two is by the vertical gap or seam over the nose that identifies it as an isolated cab-equipped SD75I that is missing on the SD75M. On 14 April 1997, a trio of Canadian National SD75I locomotives power train 340 on a detour over Wisconsin Central at Rugby, Wisconsin.

SD75I—1996–99 The biggest customer for EMD's SD75I is by far the Canadian National with 175 SD75Is, while BNSF added twenty-six to its fleet, and Ontario Northland acquired six. BNSF SD75Is that were delivered in 1997 were dressed in Santa Fe's famous red and silver Warbonnet colors and numbered 8276 to 8301. These units were eventually renumbered down into the 200s following Santa Fe/BNSF SD75M Nos 200 to 275. Repainted in a current BNSF color scheme, SD75I No. 282 basks in the morning sun just south of Bill, Wyoming, on 5 July 2019.

SD90MAC-H—1996–99 The long-awaited EMD 265H 6,000 hp engine finally made its debut in September 1996. The SD90MAC-H can be identified by dual exhaust stacks of the twin-turbo 265H engine, and beveled edges on the hood over the engine compartment. Preproduction units spent time in Colorado doing some high-altitude testing on Union Pacific's Moffat Tunnel Subdivision and a stint at the AARs Transportation Test Center in Pueblo. Here, UP SD90MAC-H No. 8503, along with 8502, 8505 and 8504, is being put through its paces at Plainview on 3 February 1998.

SD90MAC-H—1996–99 EMD's SD90MAC-H locomotives, along with EMD's test car, head through Rocky, Colorado, for some testing at Plainview on 2 February 1998. Leading the way is No. 8504, painted in a special scheme for EMD's seventy-fifth anniversary. The other three SD90MAC-Hs fully painted for Union Pacific are Nos 8505, 8502 and 8503 (west to east). After some stationary trials at Plainview and East Portal, the four will be further appraised on tonnage between Denver and the Moffat Tunnel. Despite all the preproduction testing, the SD90MAC-Hs were plagued with problems and frequently sidelined, and EMD eventually shelved the 265H and 6,000 hp locomotive.

SD70M-2—2004–11 With the Environmental Protection Agency's new Tier 2 emission standards starting 1 January 2005, EMD introduced the 16-710G3C-T2 compliant engine and a myriad of other improvements in new SD70M-2 and SD70ACe models. These two locomotives are nearly identical – with the SD70M-2 D.C. traction and SD70ACe A.C. traction. On the left side of both locomotives is a large box behind the cab. Only the SD70ACe has two elongated horizontal vents on the side of the box, which are air intake for A.C. traction equipment. Four red, white and blue Florida East Coast SD70M-2s sit near the shop at New Smyrna Beach, Florida, on 10 January 2015. FEC acquired eight SD70M-2s from EMD, but all departed the property when their leases expired in 2015.

SD70M-2—2004–11 Canadian National was a good customer for EMD's SD70M-2, buying 190 of the 4,300 hp locomotives. It's a beautiful day at Jasper, Alberta, on 20 July 2013, as Canadian National intermodal train 117 approaches milepost 8 just east of Geikie on CN's Albreda Subdivision.

SD70ACe—2004–15 The A.C. traction SD70ACe has been a popular model for EMD, with Union Pacific purchasing the largest fleet at 799 units. On 26 August 2013, Union Pacific was testing Electro-Motive Diesel's SD70ACes on the Moffat Tunnel Subdivision west of Denver, Colorado. UP's mobile laboratory car No. UPP 210 is bracketed by EMD demonstrators Nos 1206 and 1208 on high-adhesion tests with a westbound West Elk Mine coal empty leaving Rocky, Colorado.

SD70ACe—2004–15 Other good customers for the SD70ACe are BNSF, accumulating 660 units, Norfolk Southern with 225 copies and Kansas City Southern with 153 units, with seventy-five more on KCS de Mexico. KCS SD70ACe No. 4119 stands ready to lead a northbound grain train in the siding at Louise, Texas, on the bright, sunny morning of 13 March 2013.

SD70ACe—2004–15 EMD's 4,300 hp SD70ACe has even sold to some smaller railroads like Montana Rail Link with twenty-nine units, Tacoma Rail with two and Arkansas & Missouri buying a trio. On 7 May 2014, the A&M freight from Fort Smith arrives at Springdale, Arkansas, with big SD70ACe No. 72 leading the way.

SD70ACe—2004–15 An eastbound BNSF coal train descends the Front Range of the Rockies at Coal Creek Canyon east of Plainview, Colorado, on 5 May 2014. Three brand-new SD70ACes lead the train (Nos 8533, 8531 and 8530), while in the background, another new SD70ACe (No. 8532) and an older SD70MAC team up as a rear DPU locomotive set that just exited Tunnel 1.

SD70ACe-T4—2015 Led by shiny SD70ACe-T4 No. 3054, a westbound Union Pacific stack train departs Green River, Wyoming, after a crew change and begins the climb over Peru Hill on 27 September 2020. EMD's SD70ACe-T4 is a 76-foot 8-inch machine, powered by a 12-cylinder 1010 engine yielding 4,400 hp, riding on new fabricated trucks and is Tier 4 compliant. What's next for EMD? Only time will tell.